An Elizabethan House & Garden

Kathy Still
Chronicle Books

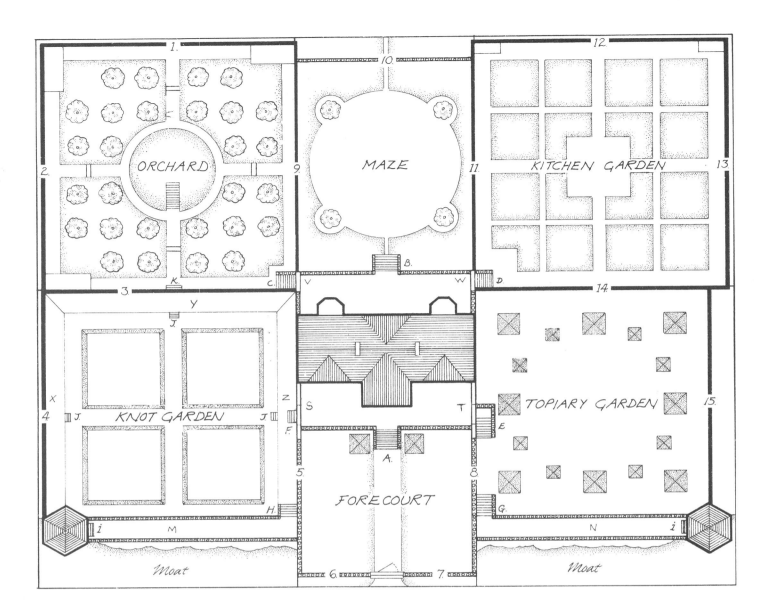

KEY TO PLAN

1–15 .... GARDEN WALLS
A–K .... FLIGHTS OF STEPS
M, N .... GARDEN TERRACES
S, T, V, W .... TERRACE ENDS
X, Y, Z .... RAISED WALKS

WHAT YOU NEED TO MAKE THE MODEL

A stout card or wooden base, size 702 mm × 570 mm (27⅝″ × 22½″). Polyboard (which is available from craft and model shops) is ideal for this purpose. Use glue or double-sided tape to fix the bases to the base-board, and a clear glue such as Uhu or Bostik 1 to make the model. You will need a craft knife, sharp scissors and a ruler.

BEFORE YOU BEGIN

Open the book flat and carefully cut the thread sewing. You will find twelve named and numbered loose sheets from which the model is made. Using scissors and/or craft knife—cut along outer rules and score along the dotted lines. Note that the fruit trees, topiary animals, fountains, sundial and people simply slot together.

RECOMMENDED METHOD

Cut out all the bases and mount them onto the baseboard. Fix the House in position before adding any of the garden walls. As this is the most difficult piece to make, you may wish to begin with some smaller pieces, such as the Dovecote, Herbs and Vegetables in the Kitchen Garden, or others which do not rely on the House or Garden walls for support. All the stone capping strips for the walls should be left aside until the rest of the model is completed.

NOTES ON CONSTRUCTION

The model is built up over seven bases—one for each of the gardens, and one for the house. The joins between bases are concealed by the flowerbed tabs on either side of the garden walls and terraces. The garden walls should be placed in alignment with the wide grey lines marked on the bases. (In common with most other pieces of the model, the flowerbed tabs are slightly bigger than the white areas they adhere to.)

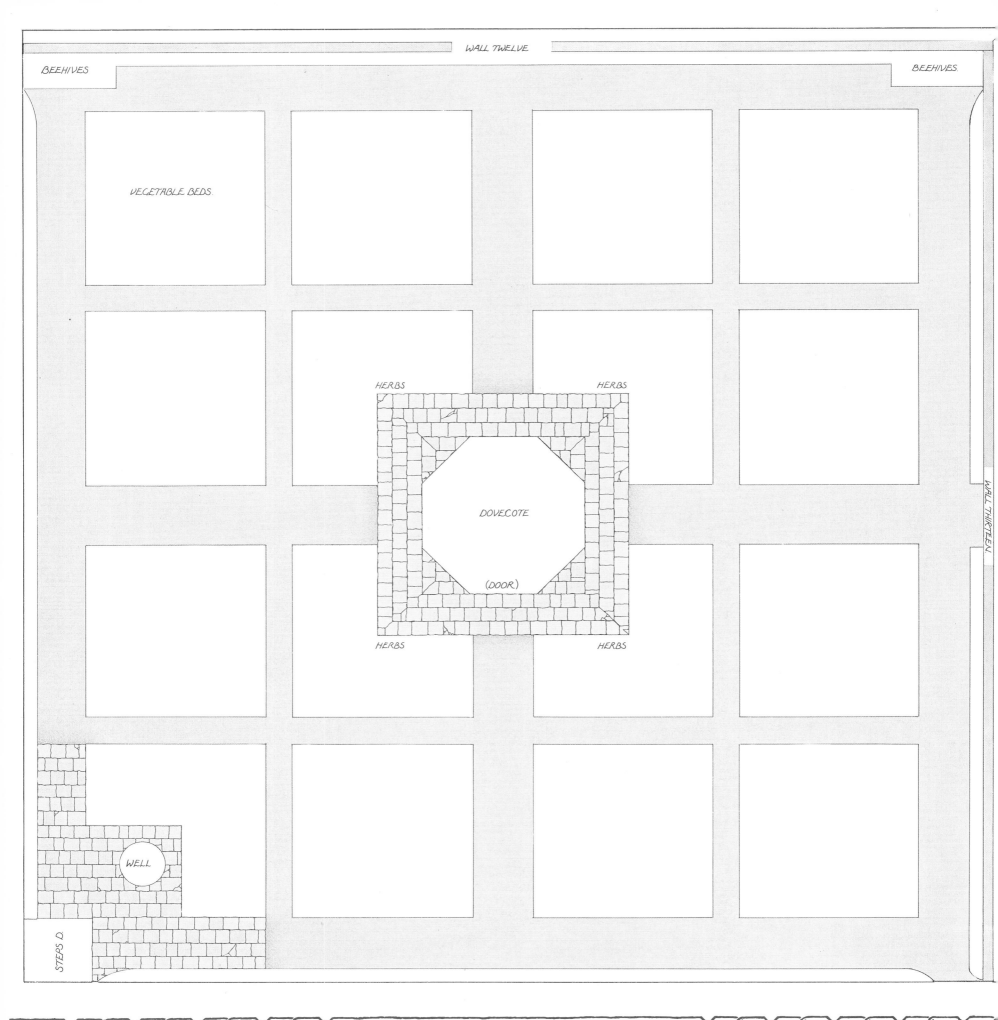

WALL TWELVE

BEEHIVES   BEEHIVES.

VEGETABLE BEDS.

WALL THIRTEEN.

HERBS   HERBS

DOVECOTE

(DOOR)

HERBS   HERBS

WELL

STEPS D.

1. The Kitchen Garden Base

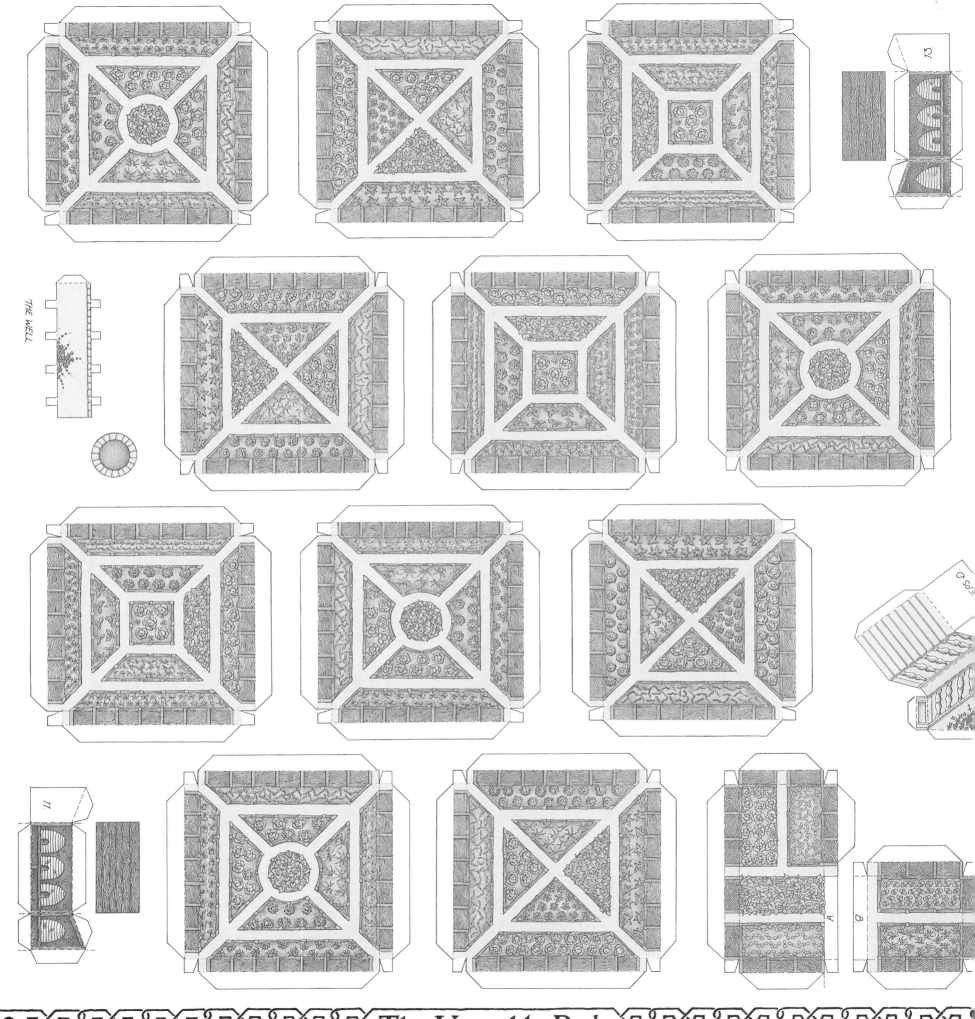

THE WELL.

2. The Vegetable Beds

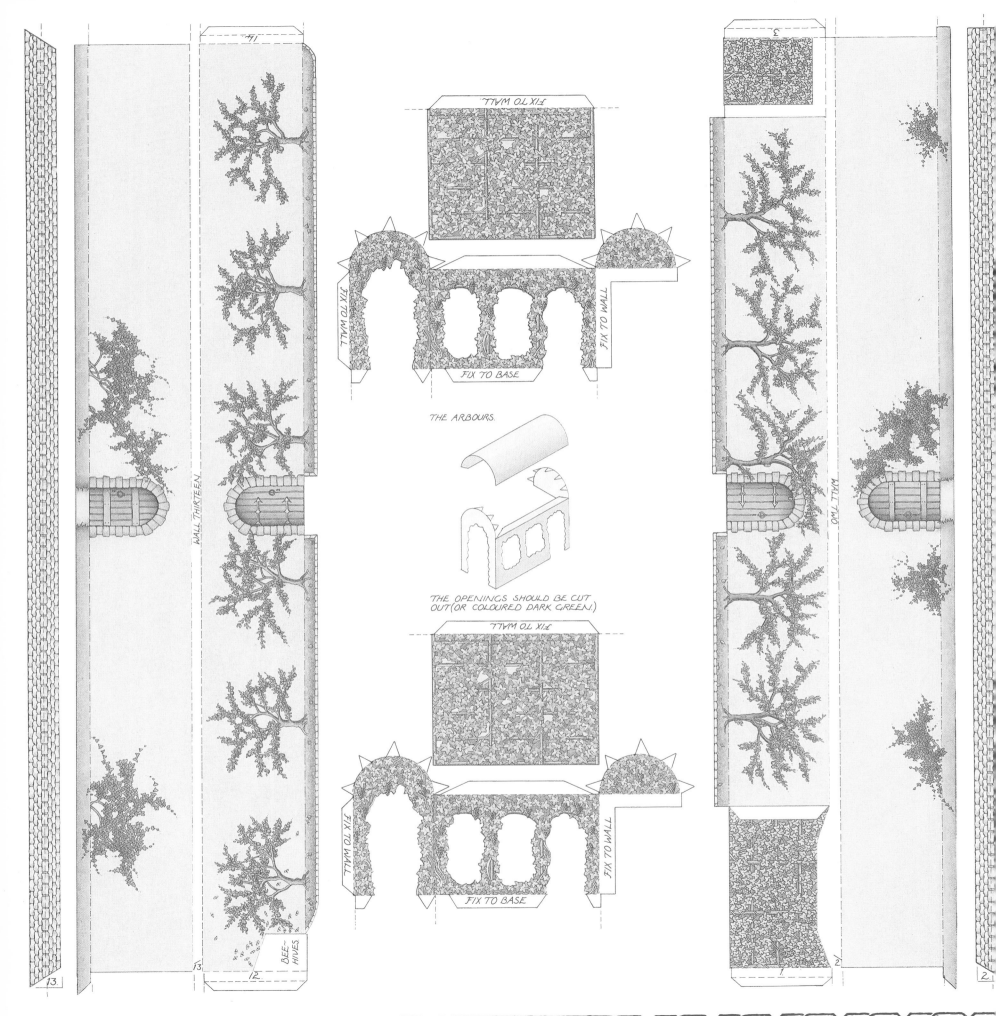

THE ARBOURS.

THE OPENINGS SHOULD BE CUT OUT (OR COLOURED DARK GREEN.)

FIX TO WALL

FIX TO BASE

FIX TO WALL

WALL THIRTEEN

WALL TWO

BEE-HIVES

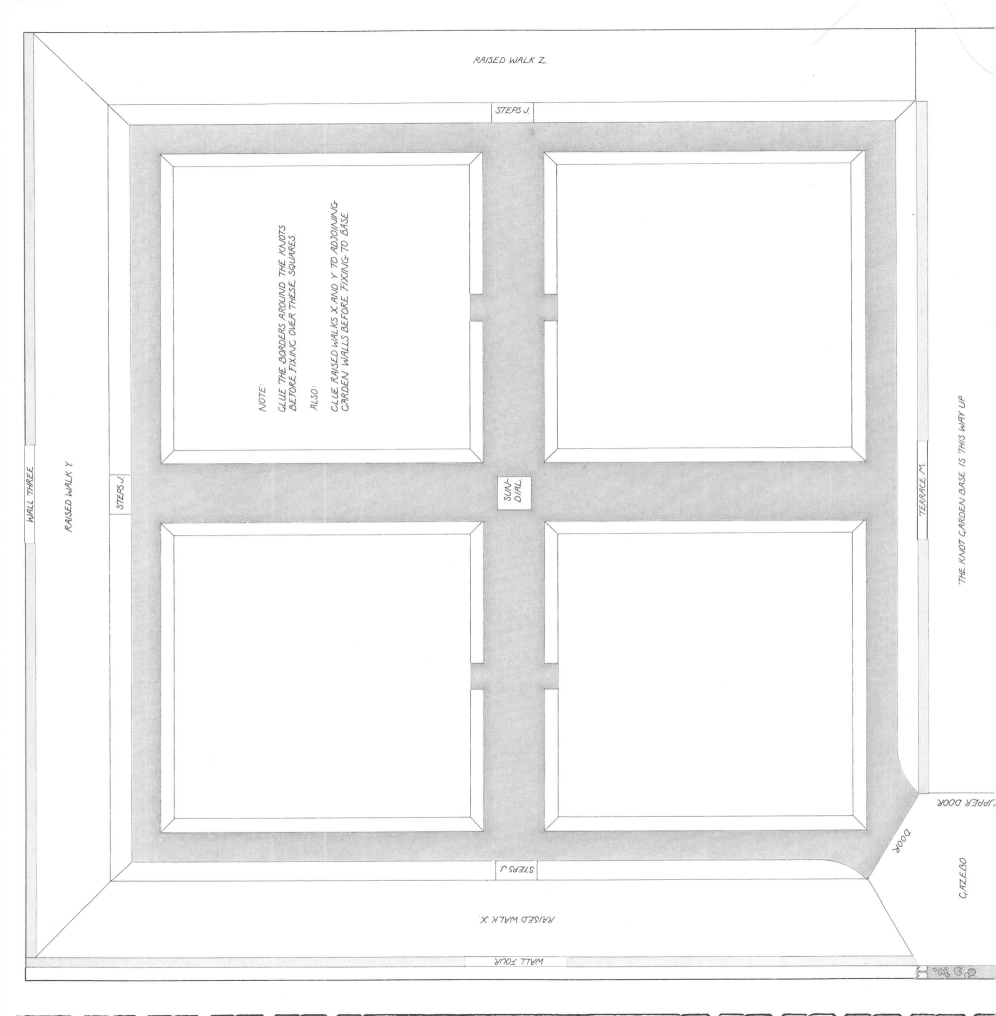

RAISED WALK Z.

STEPS J.

WALL THREE

RAISED WALK Y

STEPS J.

NOTE:

GLUE THE BORDERS AROUND THE KNOTS
BEFORE FIXING OVER THESE SQUARES.

ALSO:

GLUE RAISED WALKS X AND Y TO ADJOINING
GARDEN WALLS BEFORE FIXING TO BASE.

SUN-
DIAL.

TERRACE M.

THE KNOT GARDEN BASE IS THIS WAY UP.

UPPER DOOR

DOOR

GAZEBO

STEPS J.

RAISED WALK X.

WALL FOUR

4. The Knot Garden Base

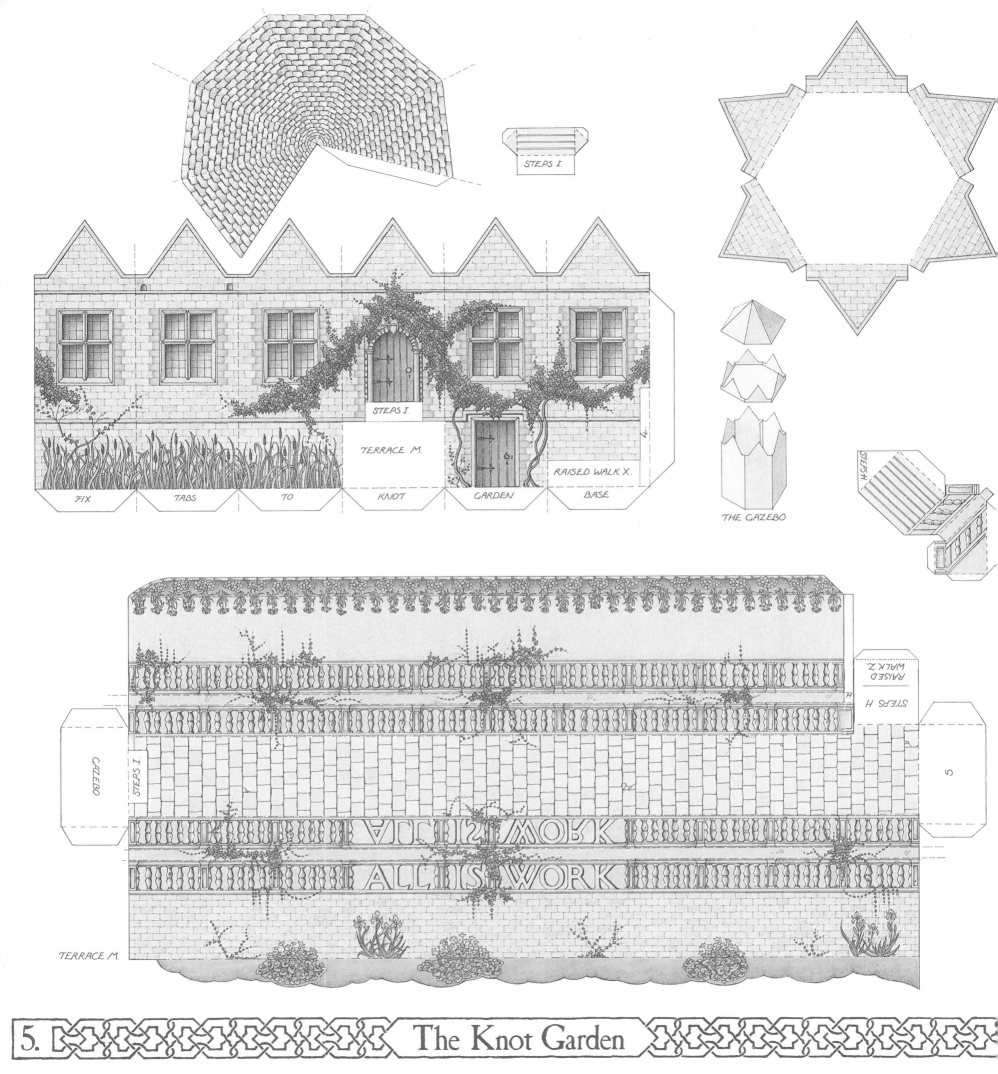

STEPS I.

STEPS I.

TERRACE M.

RAISED WALK X.

FIX TABS TO KNOT GARDEN BASE

THE GAZEBO

STEPS H.

RAISED WALK Z.

STEPS H

GAZEBO

STEPS I.

ALL IS WORK

ALL IS WORK

TERRACE M.

5

The Knot Garden

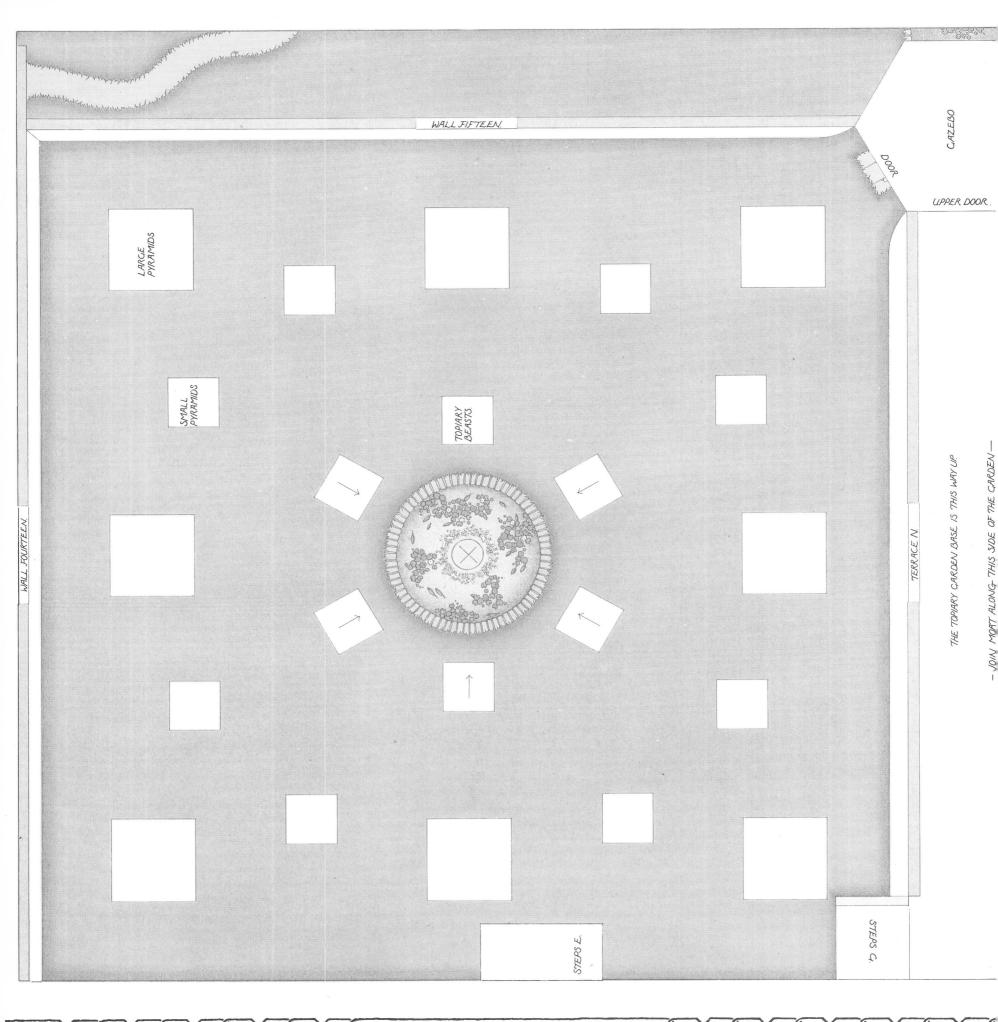

WALL FIFTEEN.

CAZEBO

DOOR

UPPER DOOR.

LARGE PYRAMIDS

SMALL PYRAMIDS

TOPIARY BEASTS.

WALL FOURTEEN.

TERRACE N.

THE TOPIARY GARDEN BASE IS THIS WAY UP

— JOIN MORT ALONG THIS SIDE OF THE GARDEN —

STEPS E.

STEPS C.

6. The Topiary Garden Base

CUT SLOTS IN CUBES AS
INDICATED. ASSEMBLE
TOPIARY BEASTS (PAGE 12)
AND SLOT INTO CUBES. FOLD
BACK TABS AND GLUE.

7. Topiary

FRONT TERRACE FLOWERBEDS........

........OVERLAP HERE

STEPS A.

TOPIARY PYRAMID

TOPIARY PYRAMID

WALL FIVE

WALL EIGHT

WALL SIX.

GATE

WAY

WALL SEVEN.

RAISED WALK X.

FIX TO GAZEBO

WALL FOUR

5

8

MAIN GATE

MAIN GATE

WALL SIX.

WALL SEVEN.

8. The Forecourt Base

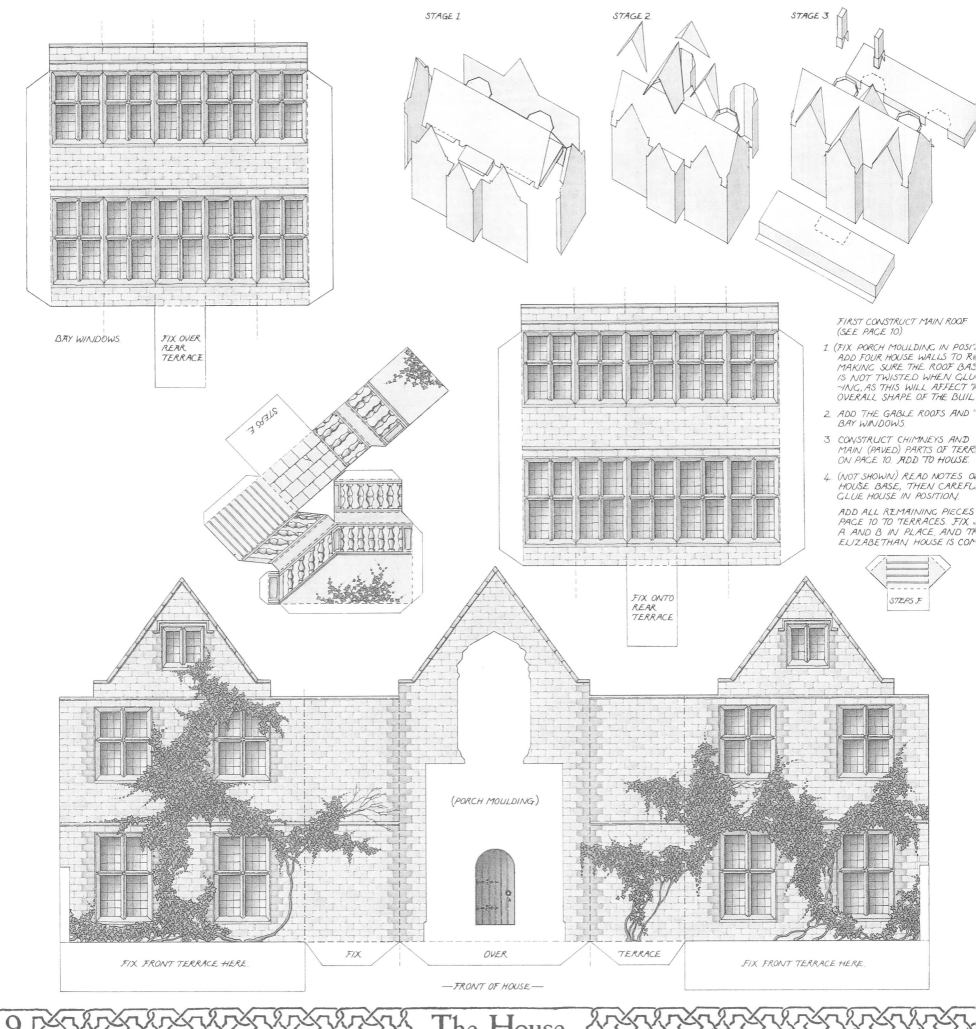

BAY WINDOWS.

FIX OVER
REAR
TERRACE

STAGE 1

STAGE 2

STAGE 3

STEPS E.

FIRST CONSTRUCT MAIN ROOF.
(SEE PAGE 10).

1. (FIX PORCH MOULDING IN POSIT?
   ADD FOUR HOUSE WALLS TO R~
   MAKING SURE THE ROOF BAS
   IS NOT TWISTED WHEN GLU
   ~ING, AS THIS WILL AFFECT T
   OVERALL SHAPE OF THE BUIL

2. ADD THE GABLE ROOFS AND T
   BAY WINDOWS.

3. CONSTRUCT CHIMNEYS AND T
   MAIN (PAVED) PARTS OF TERR
   ON PAGE 10. ADD TO HOUSE.

4. (NOT SHOWN) READ NOTES O
   HOUSE BASE, THEN CAREFU
   GLUE HOUSE IN POSITION.

   ADD ALL REMAINING PIECES
   PAGE 10 TO TERRACES. FIX
   A AND B IN PLACE, AND T
   ELIZABETHAN HOUSE IS COM

STEPS F.

FIX ONTO
REAR
TERRACE

(PORCH MOULDING)

FIX FRONT TERRACE HERE.   FIX   OVER   TERRACE   FIX FRONT TERRACE HERE.

—FRONT OF HOUSE—

9. The House

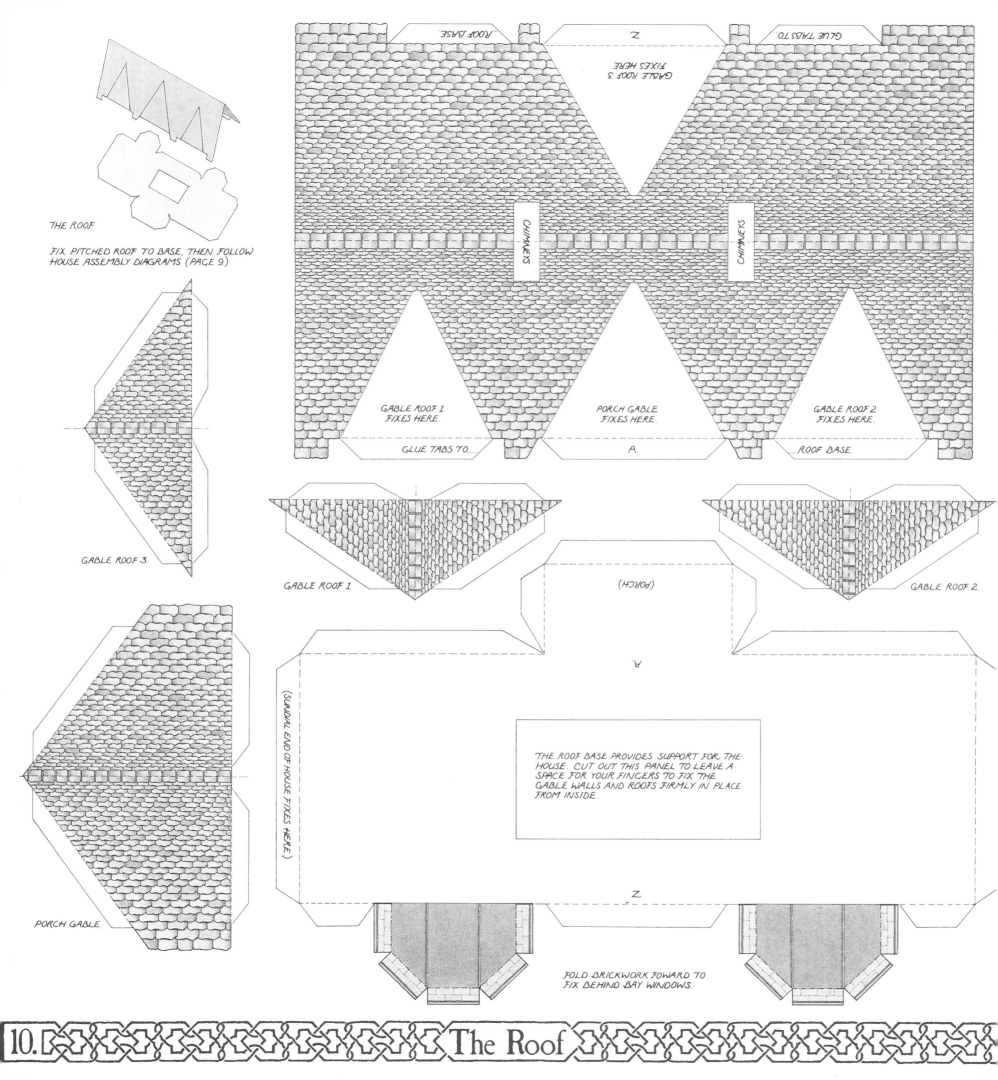

THE ROOF.

FIX PITCHED ROOF TO BASE, THEN FOLLOW
HOUSE ASSEMBLY DIAGRAMS (PAGE 9)

GABLE ROOF 3.

PORCH GABLE.

ROOF BASE.

GLUE TABS TO.... GABLE ROOF 3 FIXES HERE. Z.

CHIMNEYS

CHIMNEYS

GABLE ROOF 1. FIXES HERE.

PORCH GABLE. FIXES HERE.

GABLE ROOF 2. FIXES HERE.

GLUE TABS TO.... A. ....ROOF BASE.

GABLE ROOF 1.

(PORCH)

GABLE ROOF 2.

(SUNDIAL END OF HOUSE FIXES HERE.)

A.

THE ROOF BASE PROVIDES SUPPORT FOR THE
HOUSE. CUT OUT THIS PANEL TO LEAVE A
SPACE FOR YOUR FINGERS TO FIX THE
GABLE WALLS AND ROOFS FIRMLY IN PLACE
FROM INSIDE.

Z.

FOLD BRICKWORK FORWARD TO
FIX BEHIND BAY WINDOWS.

REAR TERRACE FLOWERBEDS

OVERLAP HERE

STEPS B

WALL ELEVEN

WALL NINE

-THIS WAY UP

WALL TEN

THE MAZE IS-

FIX MULBERRY TREES OVER CROSSES AND FOUNTAIN IN CENTRE (ALL ON PAGE TWELVE).

10

11

12

BEE-
HIVES

WALL ELEVEN

The Maze Base

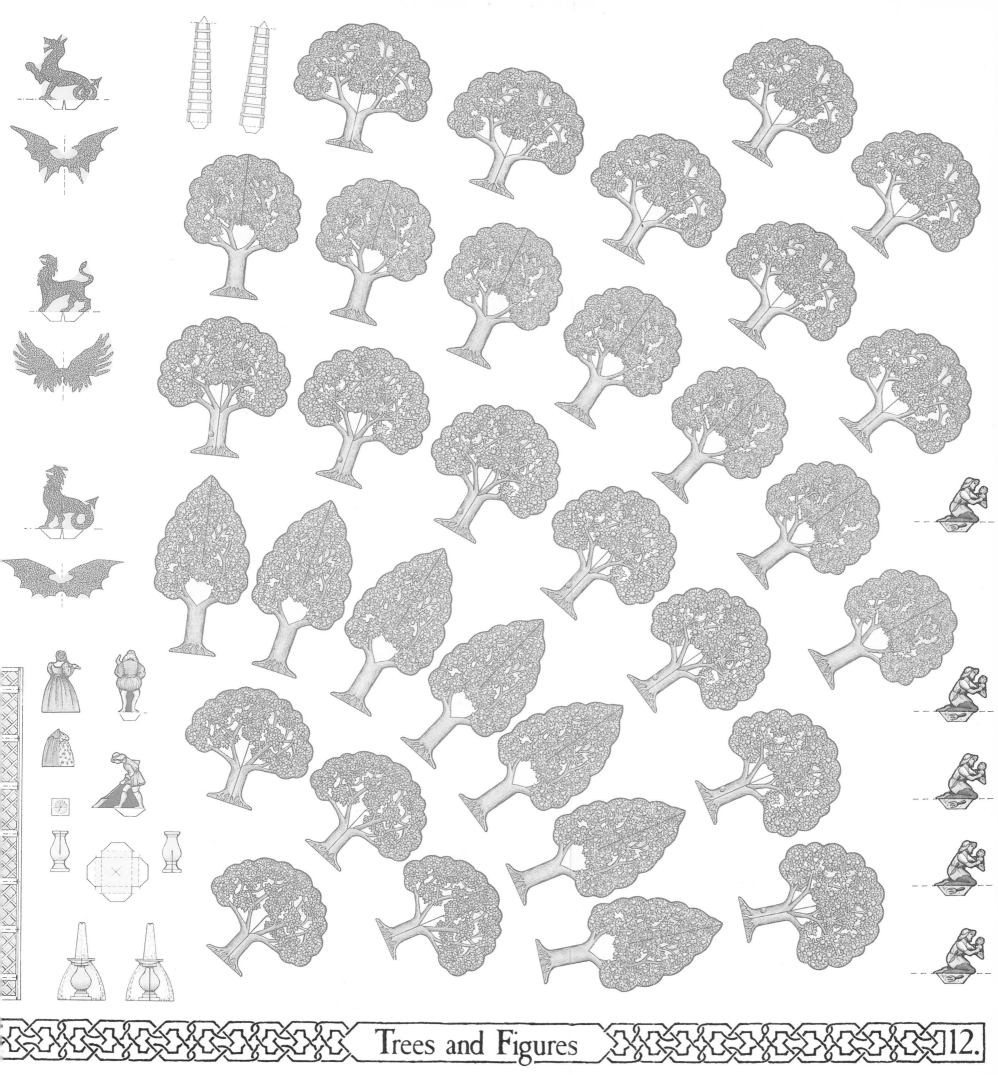

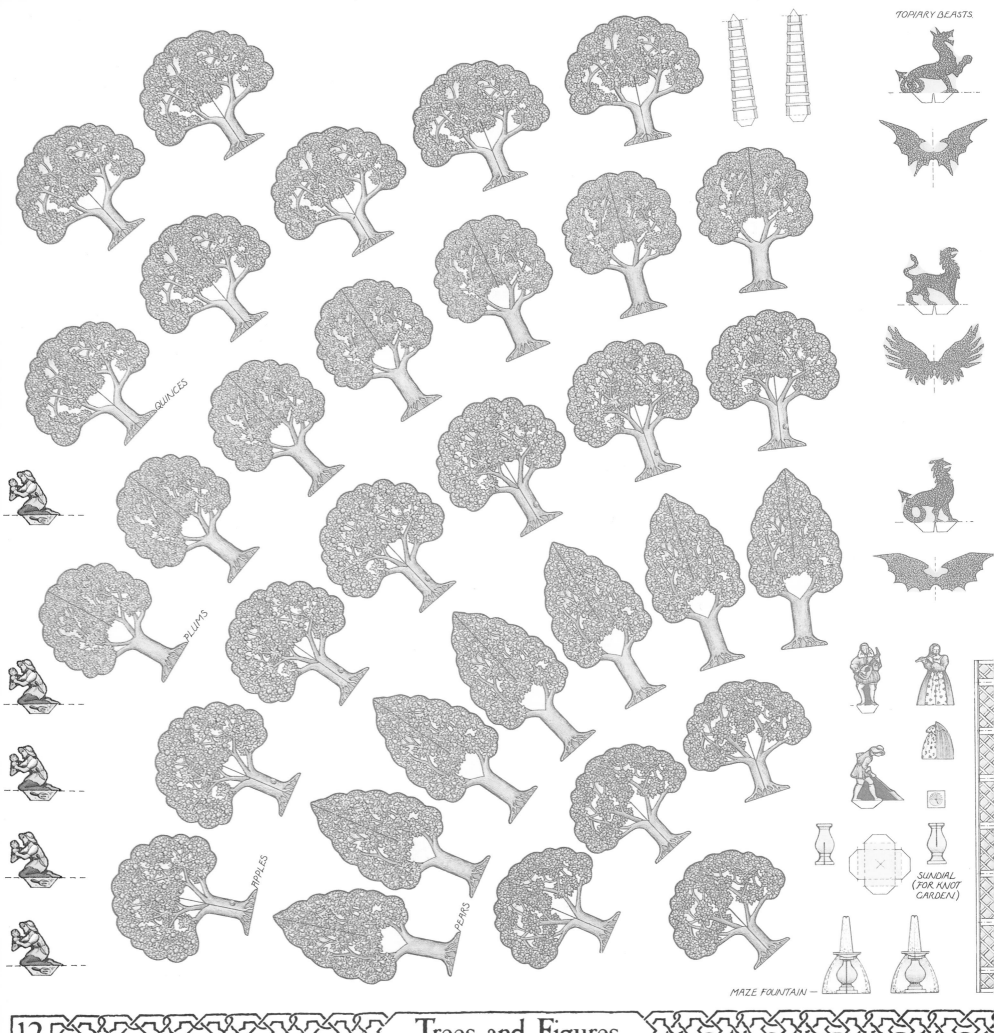

QUINCES

PLUMS

APPLES

PEARS

SUNDIAL
(FOR KNOT
GARDEN.)

MAZE FOUNTAIN —

12. Trees and Figures

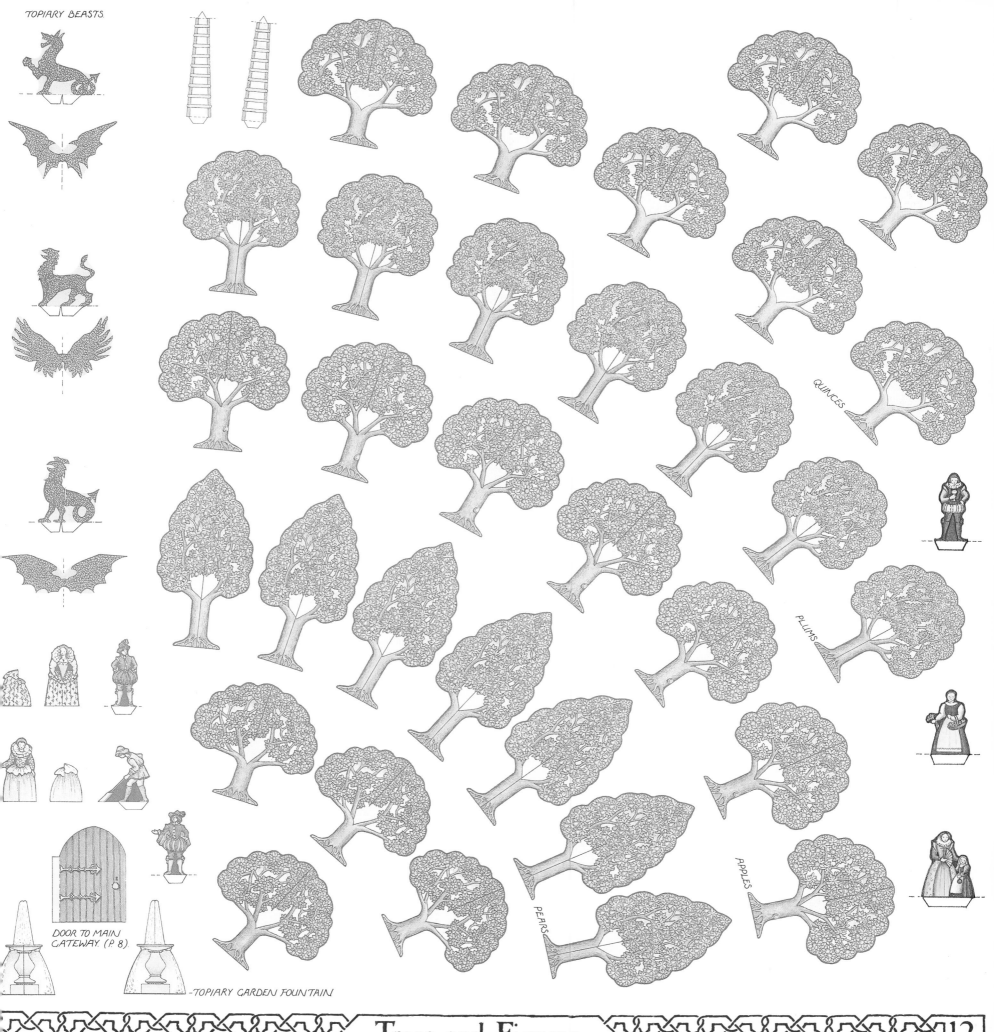

TOPIARY BEASTS.

QUINCES

PLUMS

APPLES

PEARS

DOOR TO MAIN
GATEWAY. (P. 8).

TOPIARY GARDEN FOUNTAIN.

Trees and Figures

12.

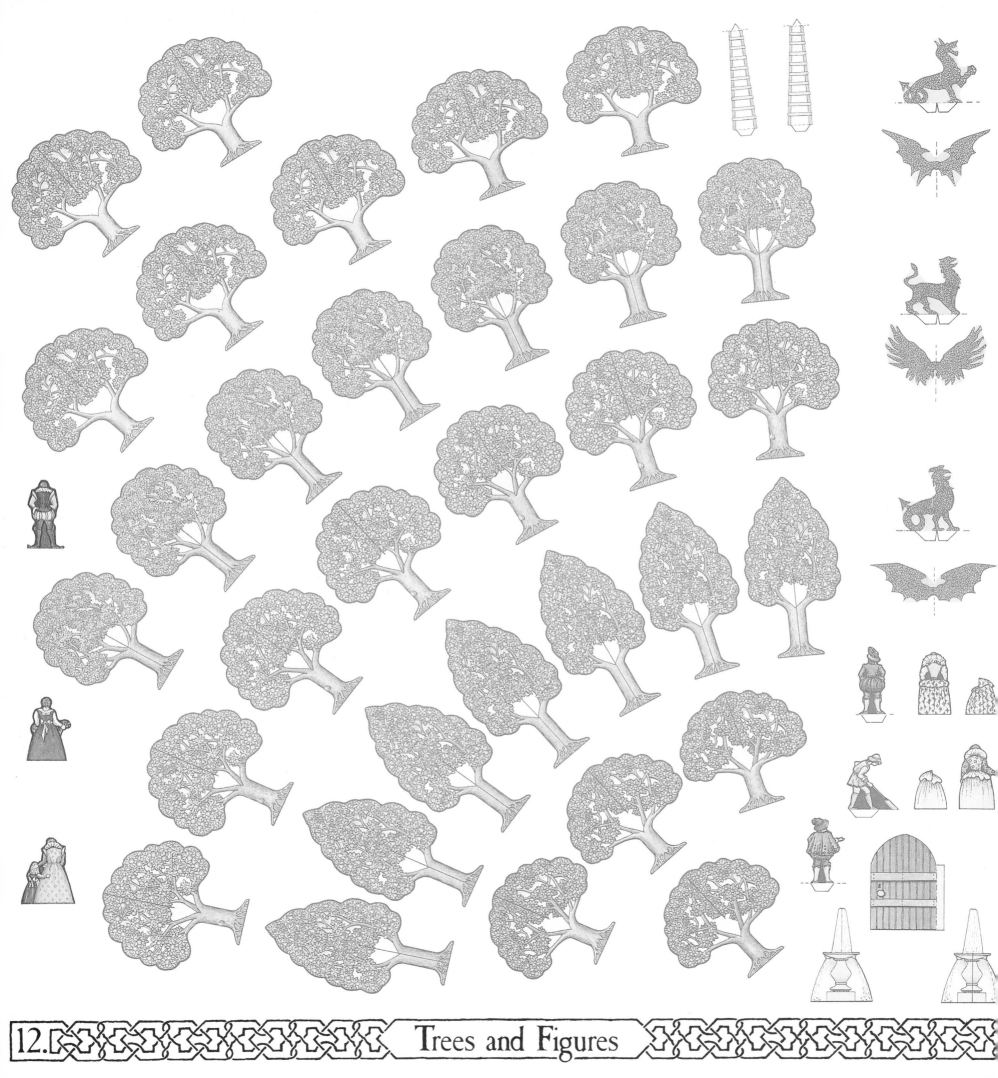

Trees and Figures

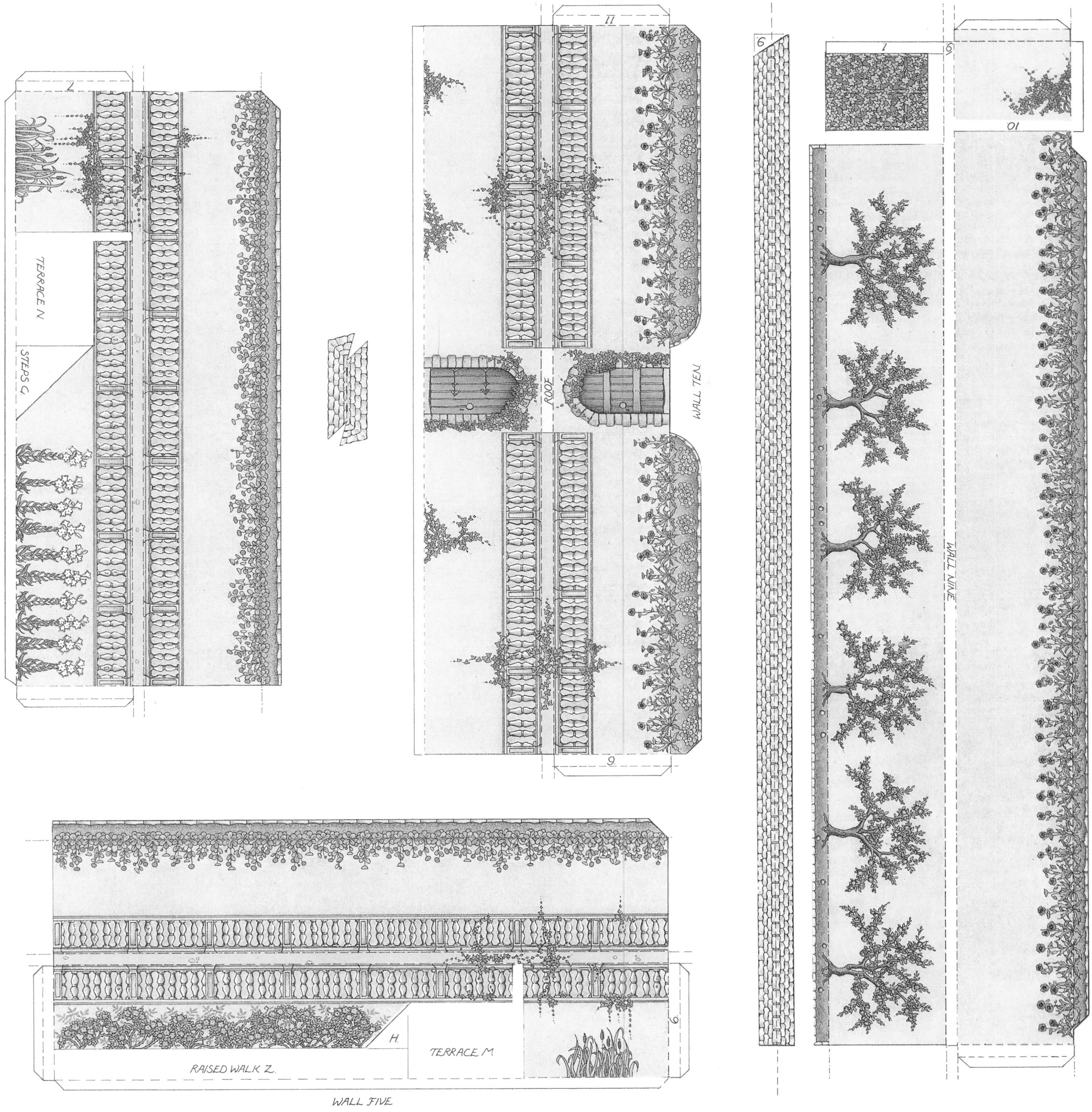

WALL EIGHT

2

TERRACE N

STEPS G.

11

ROOF

WALL TEN

9

6

1 6

01

WALL NINE

RAISED WALK Z.

H.

TERRACE M

6

WALL FIVE

11.

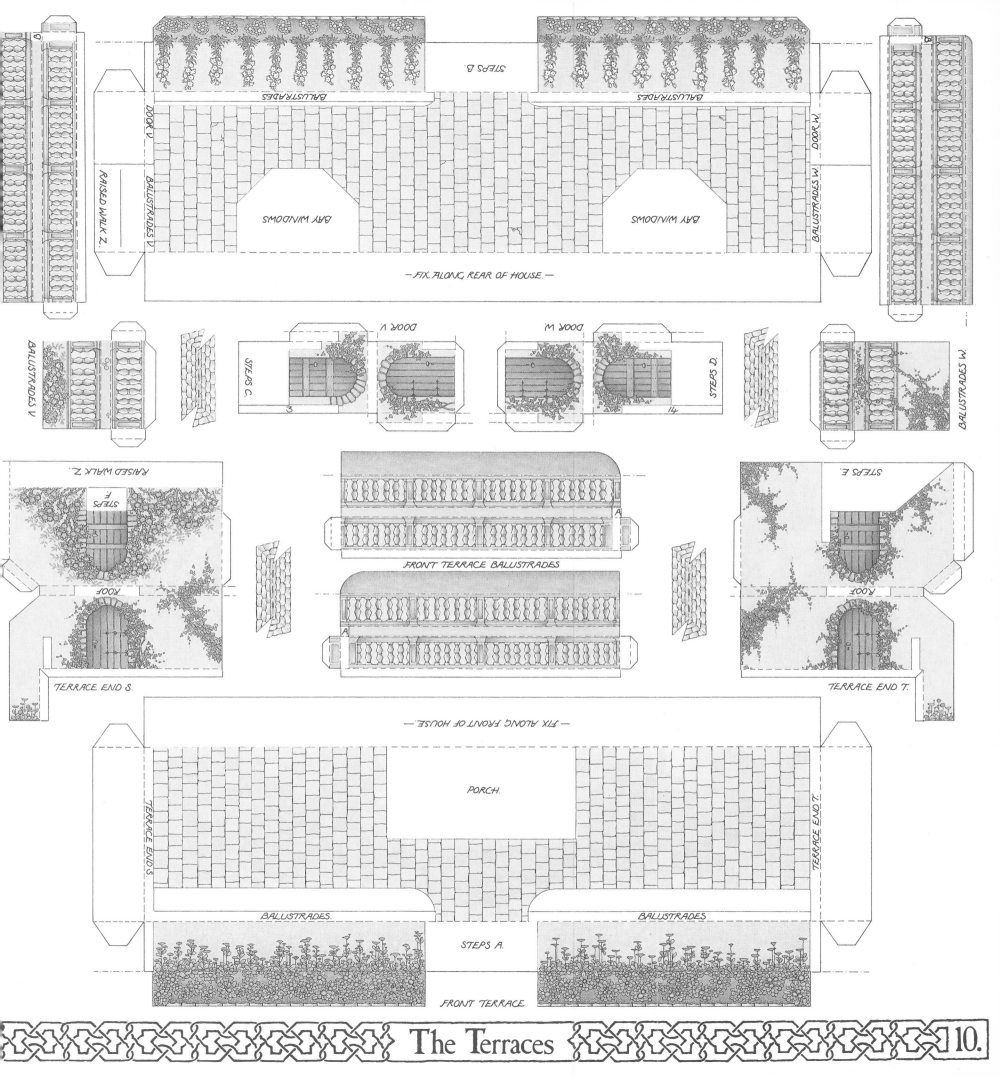

STEPS B.

BALUSTRADES

BALUSTRADES

DOOR V

DOOR W

RAISED WALK Z.

BALUSTRADES V

BALUSTRADES W

BALUSTRADES W

BAY WINDOWS

BAY WINDOWS

— FIX ALONG, REAR OF HOUSE.—

BALUSTRADES V

DOOR V

DOOR W

STEPS C.

STEPS D.

BALUSTRADES W

RAISED WALK Z.

STEPS E.

STEPS F

ROOF

FRONT TERRACE BALUSTRADES

ROOF

TERRACE END S.

TERRACE END T.

— FIX ALONG FRONT OF HOUSE.—

TERRACE END S.

PORCH.

TERRACE END T.

BALUSTRADES.

BALUSTRADES

STEPS A.

FRONT TERRACE

The Terraces

10.

BALUSTRADED STEPS
A AND B.

STEPS A

FIX TO REAR OF HOUSE.

FIX TO FRONT OF HOUSE.

FIX TO FRONT OF HOUSE.

FIX TO REAR OF HOUSE.

OVID THE NIGHT

GLUE TO BASE

RAISED WALK Z.

GLUE TO BASE

STEPS A.

CHIMNEYS

CUT OUT

PORCH MOULDING.

BAY WINDOWS

CUT OUT

BAY WINDOWS

CUT OUT

— FIX REAR TERRACE ALONG HERE —
(CUT OUT RECTANGLES IN ORDER TO FIX BAY WINDOWS OVER REAR TERRACE – STAGE 3).

CHIMNEYS.

The House

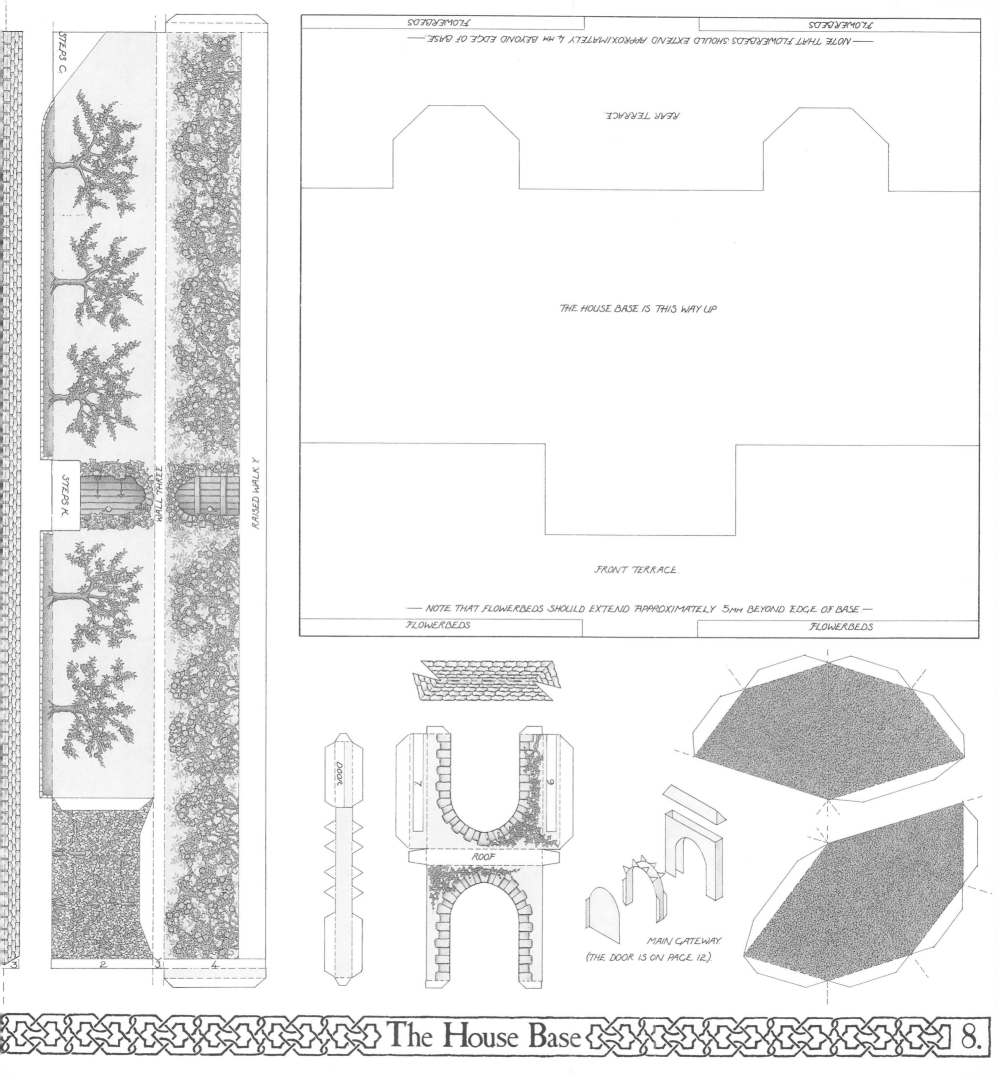

STEPS C.

STEPS THREE

WALL THREE

RAISED WALK Y.

3

2

3

4

— NOTE THAT FLOWERBEDS SHOULD EXTEND APPROXIMATELY 4 MM BEYOND EDGE OF BASE —

REAR TERRACE.

THE HOUSE BASE IS THIS WAY UP

FRONT TERRACE.

— NOTE THAT FLOWERBEDS SHOULD EXTEND APPROXIMATELY 5 MM BEYOND EDGE OF BASE —

FLOWERBEDS

FLOWERBEDS

DOOR

7

6

ROOF

MAIN GATEWAY.

(THE DOOR IS ON PAGE 12).

The House Base

8.

ASSEMBLE THE PIECES
SEPERATELY, THEN GLUE
CORRESPONDING TABS
P.Q.R ON KNOTS
AND BORDERS. THE
UNLETTERED TABS
FIX TO THE BASE.

Knots

7.

JOIN MOAT TO TOPIARY GARDEN BASE.

TERRACE N.

WALL FOURTEEN

STEPS D

WALL FIFTEEN

FIX TO GAZEBO

6.

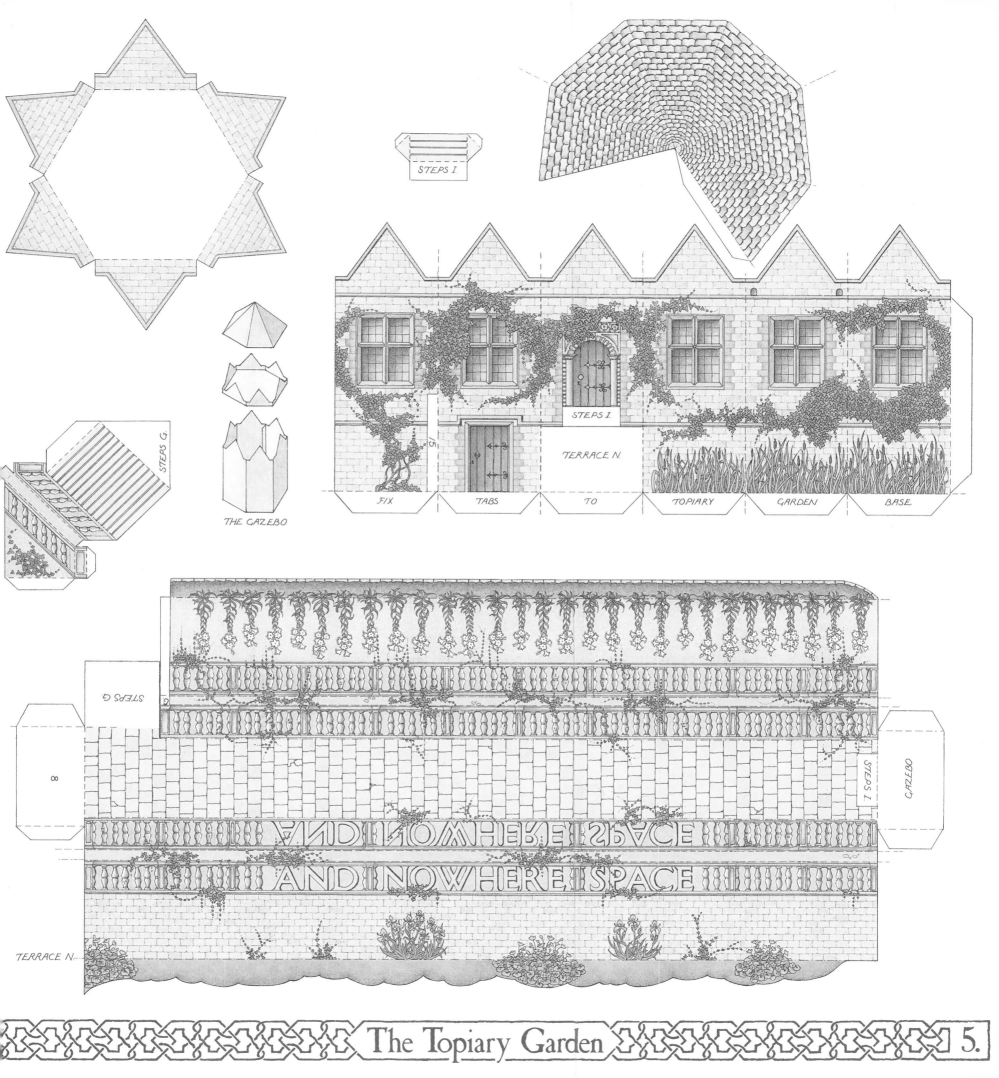

STEPS I.

STEPS G.

THE GAZEBO

STEPS I.

TERRACE N.

FIX   TABS   TO   TOPIARY   GARDEN   BASE

STEPS G.

8

STEPS I.

GAZEBO

AND NOWHERE SPACE

AND NOWHERE SPACE

TERRACE N.

The Topiary Garden   5.

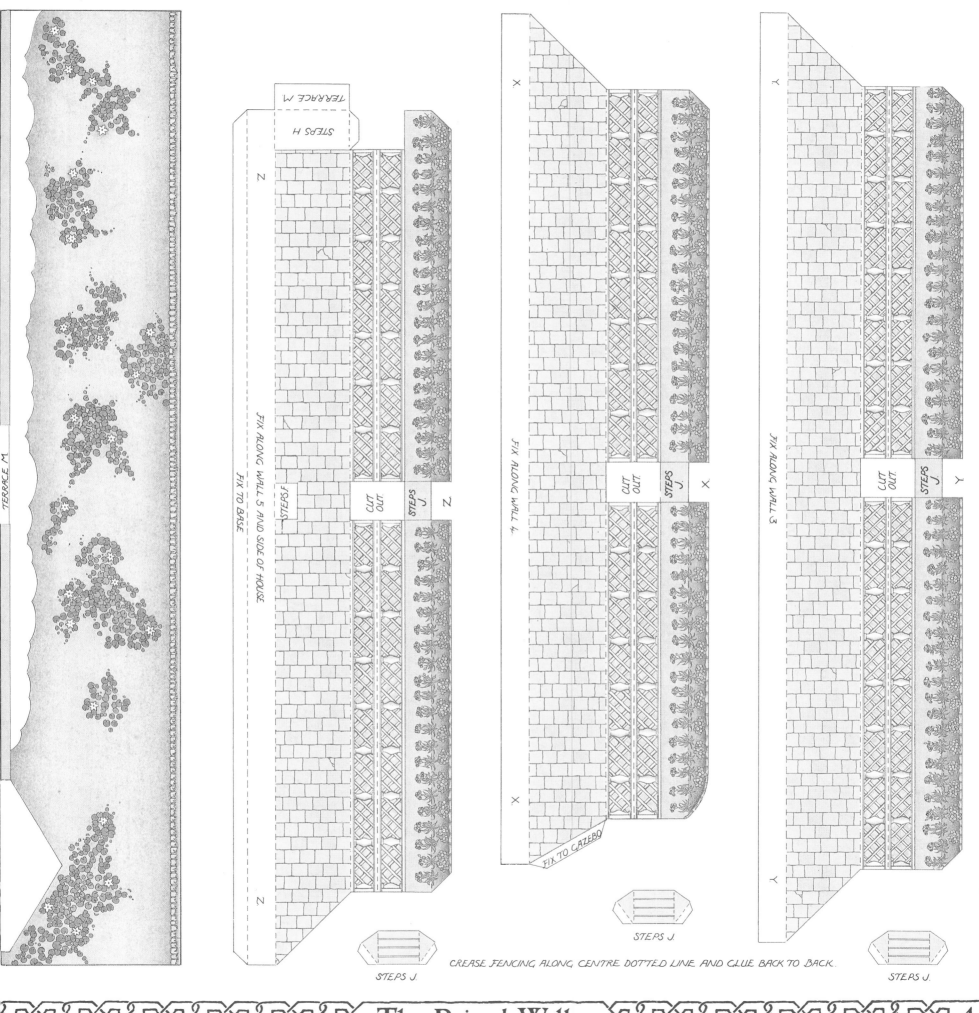

TERRACE M

STEPS H
TERRACE M
STEPS F
FIX ALONG WALL 5 AND SIDE OF HOUSE
FIX TO BASE
Z
Z
Z
CUT OUT.
STEPS J
Z

STEPS J.

X
X
X
FIX ALONG WALL 4.
CUT OUT.
STEPS J
X
FIX TO GAZEBO

STEPS J.

Y
Y
Y
FIX ALONG WALL 3
CUT OUT.
STEPS J
Y

STEPS J.

CREASE FENCING ALONG CENTRE DOTTED LINE AND GLUE BACK TO BACK.

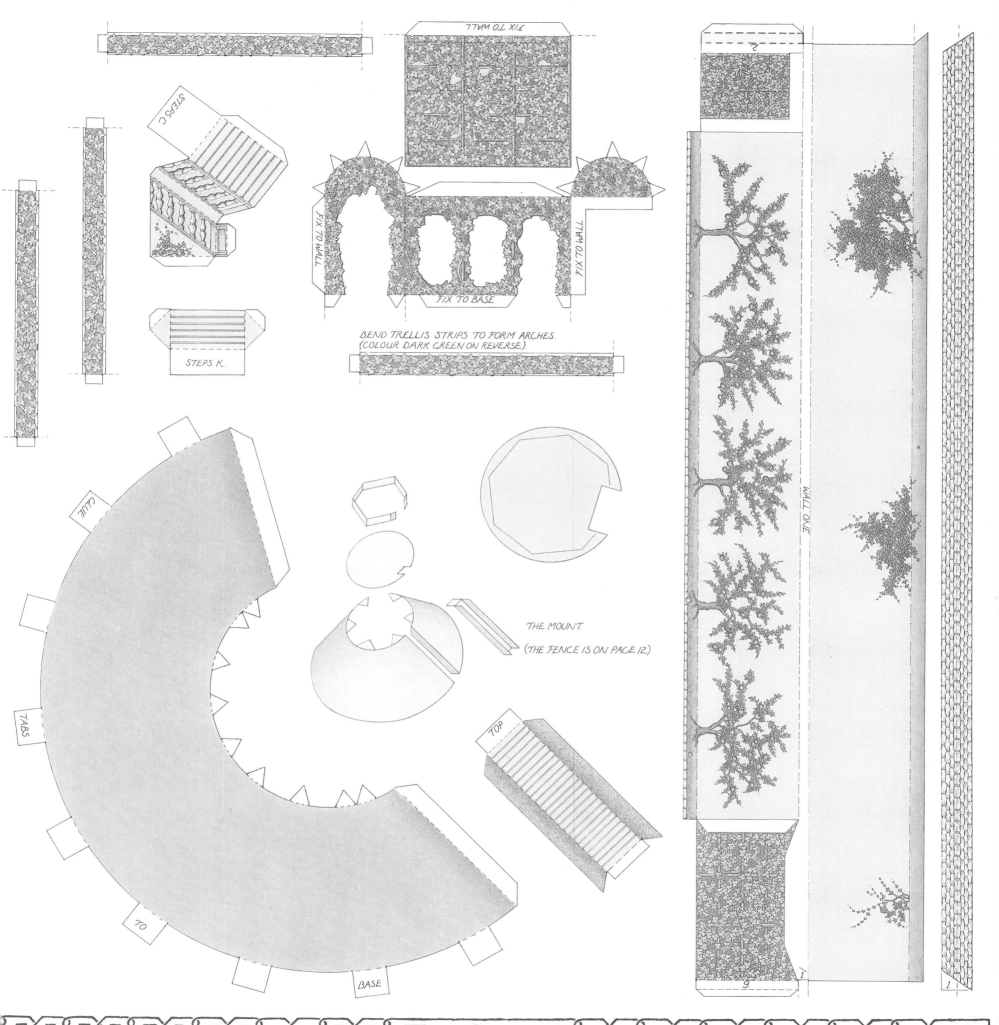

STEPS C.

FIX TO WALL

FIX TO WALL

FIX TO WALL

FIX TO WALL

FIX TO BASE

BEND TRELLIS STRIPS TO FORM ARCHES.
(COLOUR DARK GREEN ON REVERSE.)

STEPS K.

GLUE

TABS

TO

BASE

THE MOUNT.

(THE FENCE IS ON PAGE 12.)

TOP

WALL ONE

The Orchard

3.

BEEHIVES.

WALL TWELVE

BEEHIVES

FIX TO   KITCHEN   GARDEN   BASE

GLUE TOGETHER TABS A AND B TO
COMPLETE THE HERB BEDS.

A.

B

A

B

A

B

A

THE DOVECOTE

The Kitchen Garden   2.

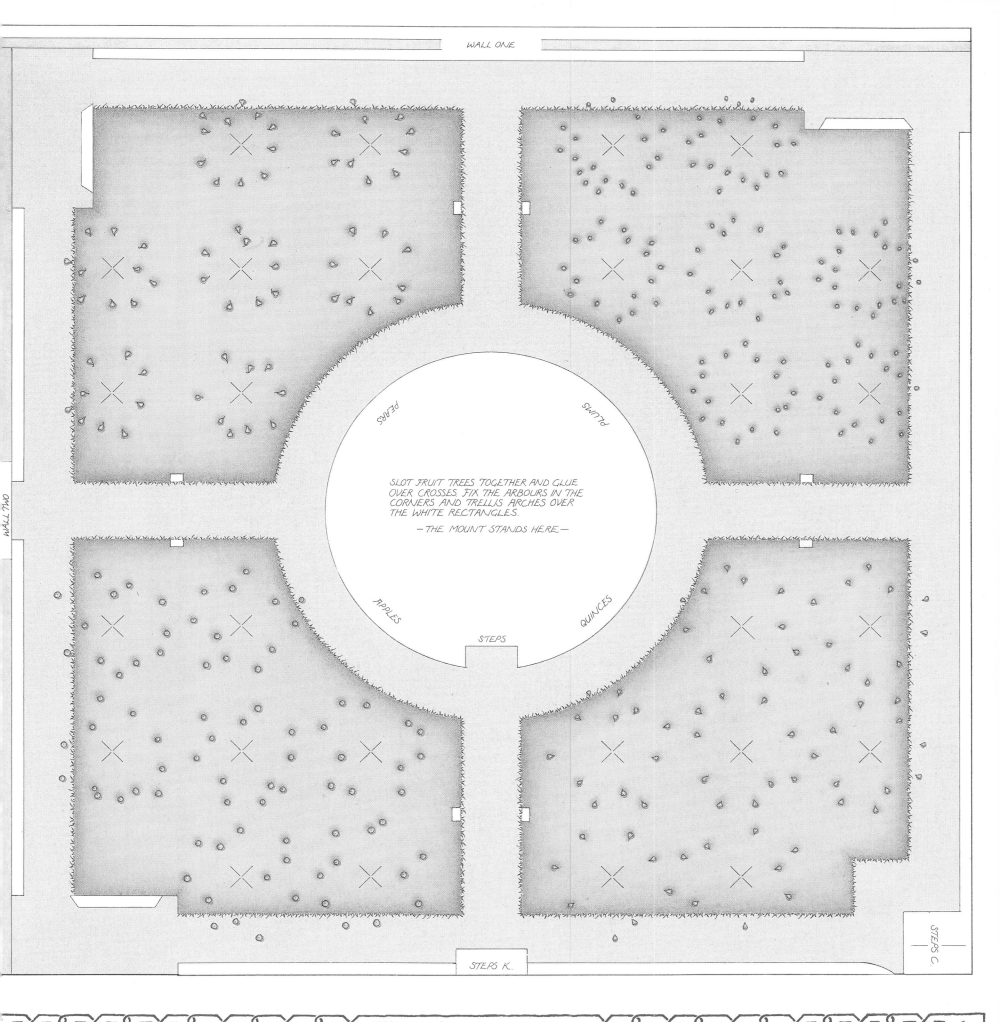

WALL TWO

PEARS

PLUMS

SLOT FRUIT TREES TOGETHER AND GLUE
OVER CROSSES. FIX THE ARBOURS IN THE
CORNERS AND TRELLIS ARCHES OVER
THE WHITE RECTANGLES.

— THE MOUNT STANDS HERE —

APPLES

QUINCES

STEPS

STEPS K.

STEPS C.

The Orchard Base

1.

The Orchard

The Knot Garden

The pieces and . . .

The Maze

The House

The Forecourt

The Kitchen Garden

The Topiary Garden

. . . where to find them

All droops, all dies, all trodden under dust,
The person, place and passages forgotten;
The hardest steel eaten with softest rust,
The firm and solid tree both rent and rotten.

FROM '*The Ocean's Love to Cynthia*' By SIR WALTER RALEIGH.

'Who would therefore looke dangerously up at Planets, that might safely looke downe at Plants?'

– Gerard's *Herbal*, 1597

The book

The last section can be pulled out and folded to make a 32-page book. Cut the whole section along the solid line printed on the first page, fold along the dotted lines, assemble the pages in numerical order by inserting one section into the middle of the other section. You will find the cover of the book is printed in colour and faces the last section. Place the cover around the folded section, then stitch together as shown in the diagram below.

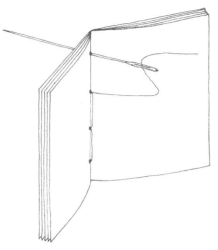

Acknowledgements

I am grateful to everyone who has been involved with the 'Elizabethan House and Garden' during its lengthy evolution. Special thanks are due to my husband, Chris Sampson, for all his help, support and remarkable tolerance. I would also like to mention Judith Elliott, who has given me so much advice and encouragement, and Bob Christie, who has taken great care over the production of this book.

Now stand you on the top of happy hours,

An Elizabethan House & Garden

Much liker than your painted counterfeit.

With virtuous wish would bear your living flowers,

Kathy Still
Chronicle Books

The first ever English gardening manual, entitled *The Gardener's Labyrinth*, was published in 1571. Its author, Thomas Hill, gives advice on all manner of topics, from such down-to-earth matters as the dunging of gardens to the influence of the stars, moon and planets on various gardening operations.

Vegetables had been grown together with herbs and flowers, but now a distinction was made and they were banished to a separate kitchen garden. Various new vegetables, such as melons and artichokes as well as improved strains of the traditional ones, were grown in the gardens of the gentry. Many of the original seeds and roots had been introduced by refugees from Flanders, who established market gardens in Kent and East Anglia.

Edible herbs and roots such as leeks, onions, parsnips and coleworts were known as 'potherbs'. They were eaten boiled and buttered, roasted in the embers, or added to 'pottages' with all kinds of less familiar greenstuff gathered from the fields and hedgerows. The gentry ate few vegetables apart from 'sallets' and those considered rare or delicate, but consumed vast quantities of meat, fish and fowl.

Part of the country gentleman's day would be devoted to the running of his estate, while the lady of the manor would be responsible for the garden and household. The main meal began at eleven o'clock, and might take up as much as three hours of the day. Supper, a much less elaborate affair, was taken at six o'clock.

A gentleman's dress was artificial and flamboyant but not nearly so unwieldy as that of his wife. With the upper half of her body constricted by a stiff bodice, and the lower half encased in a huge farthingale, her progress was necessarily stately and deliberate. Many simple tasks would have presented difficulties without the aid of a more sensibly-clad servant. Both sexes wore starched ruffs, jewellery and richly embroidered garments of costly fabrics, and children were dressed as miniature adults.

Such elaborate clothes could not be washed, but there were various methods of refreshing them. One was to spread the robes over the beds of the knot-garden in the sun, so that they would be permeated with the sweet scent of the herbs. Nosegays and pomanders were a wise precaution when dealing with the lower orders in an age when personal cleanliness left much to be desired.

Houses, Manor-houses and Mansions to visit

Chastleton House, Oxfordshire (a splendid early seventeenth-century Cotswold house.)
Hardwick Hall, Derbyshire (National Trust)
Losely Park, Surrey
Montacute House, Somerset (National Trust)
Parham Park, West Sussex
Shipton Hall, Shropshire
Sulgrave Manor, Northamptonshire (the ancestral home of the Washington family)
The Shakespeare Birthplace Trust Properties, in and around Stratford on Avon, Warwickshire.
Trerice, Cornwall (National Trust)

Other houses with notable interior features include: Broughton Castle, Oxfordshire; Haddon Hall, Derbyshire; Little Moreton Hall, Cheshire (National Trust) and Sizergh Castle, Cumbria (National Trust).

For opening times and details of other properties to visit, consult the current edition of Historic Houses, Castles and gardens (British Leisure Publications).

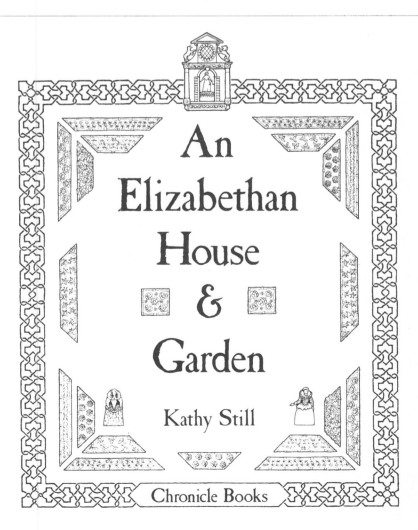

An
Elizabethan
House
&
Garden

Kathy Still

Chronicle Books

Household Management

As roads and communications were poor, the rural household had to be fairly self-sufficient. Family and servants were dependent on the mistress' skilful management of her garden, not only to provide food and medicines, but also for the seeds that would ensure next year's crop.

Much garden produce had to be kept for consumption during the winter months, and that which could not be stored was pickled, dried or preserved in honey. Since sugar was expensive, honey remained the general means of sweetening food, and bee-keeping was one of the many skills demanded of a good wife. Grapes or crab-apples were used to make verjuice, a sharp cider which was an essential ingredient of Elizabethan cookery, as were the herbs and flowers used for flavouring and colouring. Cinnamon, ginger, cloves and nutmeg were among the very few imported items.

Ornamental waters such as the moat and ponds on the model would be stocked with carp, trout and other freshwater fish. (Wednesday, Friday and Saturday were all fish-days, and meat was not eaten.) The dovecote supplied pigeons for the table – a welcome treat in winter, when fresh meat was scarce.

6

Chronicle Books
San Francisco
California

Copyright © Kathy Still, 1987
All rights reserved

Produced by Shuckburgh Reynolds Ltd
289 Westbourne Grove, London W11 2QA

Designed by Kathy Still

Printed in Spain by Graficas Estella

II

The Art of Grafting

'For to have Medlers without stones, the which shal tast swete as hony, ye shal graffe them upon an Eglentine or Sweete Brier tree, and ye shall wet the grafs (before ye graffe them) in hony.

'To colour Peache stones, that all the fruite thereof shal have the like colour hereafter, that is: ye shall lay or set Peache stones in the earth seven dayes or more, untill ye shall see the stones beginne to open, then take the stones and the curnelles softly foorth thereof, and what colour ye wil, colour the curnel therewith, and put them into the shel againe, then binde it faste togither and sette it in the earth, with the small ende upwarde, and so let him growe, and all the peaches which shall come of the same fruite (graffed or ungraffed) will be of the same colour.

'If ye put of fiery coles under an Apple tree, and then cast of the power of brimstone therein, and the fume thereof ascend up, and touch any Apple that is wet, that Apple shall fall incontinent.'

FROM *A booke of the Arte and maner, howe to plante and grafte all sortes of trees*, By LEONARD MASCALL, 1569.

19

Gardens to Visit

The following gardens are open to the public and list Knot Gardens or (reconstructed) Elizabethan Gardens among their attractions:
Barnsley House Garden, Gloucestershire
Broughton Castle, Oxfordshire
Cranborne Manor Gardens, Dorset
Hampton Court Palace, London
Holdenby House Gardens, Northamptonshire
Little Moreton Hall, Cheshire (National Trust)
New Place, Stratford on Avon, Warwickshire
Red Lodge, Bristol, Avon
Sudeley Castle, Gloucestershire
Swannington Manor Gardens, Norfolk
Tudor House Museum, Southampton, Hampshire

The Museum of Garden History (run by the Tradescant Trust) is well worth a visit. The museum is in the former church of St. Mary-at-Lambeth in South London, and a period garden has been created in the churchyard.

There is also a Garden History Society. For details write to: The Garden History Society, P.O. Box 27, Haselmere, Surrey GU27 3OJ.

27

"The tame and graffed Apple trees are planted and set in gardens and orchards made for that purpose: they delight to grow in good and fertile grounds: Kent doth abound with apples of most sorts. But I have seene in the pastures and hedge-rows about the grounds of a worshipful gentleman dwelling two miles from Hereford called Master Roger Bodnome, so many trees of all sorts, that the servants drinke for the most part no other drinke but that which is made of Apples; The quantity is such, that by the report of the Gentleman himselfe, the Parson hath for tithe many hogsheads of Syder. The hogs are fed with the fallings of them which are so many, that they make choise of those Apples they do eat, who will not taste of any but the best. An example doubtles to be followed of Gentlemen that have land and living . . . forward in the name of God, graffe, set, plant and nourish up trees in every corner of your grounds, the labour is small, the cost is nothing, the commoditie is great, your selves shall have plenty, the poore shall have somewhat in time of want to relieve their necessitie, and God shall reward your good mindes and diligence."

FROM GERARD'S *Herbal*, 1597.

18

Epilogue

Many fine Elizabethan houses, from the immense Hardwick Hall, to more modest examples of the kind illustrated by the model, can still be seen today. Interiors have inevitably been rearranged according to changing needs, but externally several remain almost unaltered.

The intimate quality of Elizabethan gardens was lost as the seventeenth century progressed, and gardens grew ever larger and more formal. Vast areas of geometric patterns were executed in grass, gravel and clipped evergreens with hardly a flower to be seen. Such tedious symmetry provoked a reaction towards the landscape style of gardening, which literally gained ground at the expense of the formal garden. Only a few architectural features survive from the Elizabethan period, the best examples being the twin gazebos and terraces at Montacute in Somerset.

The design of gardens is no longer ruled by fashion, but by economy; lawns and trees are much less troublesome than knots and topiary. Reconstructed knots have however been made in a few gardens, the best known being those at Hampton Court in Surrey, and Shakespeare's New Place at Stratford-upon-Avon.

One of the most important household offices was the stillroom. Here the essences of plants were distilled in summer and stored in flasks for later use. These were the 'active ingredients' of herbal medicine, used in making oils, powders, tinctures and 'cordial waters'. Distillations of herbs and flowers were also blended for their fragrance, which the lady of the manor would add to her home-made cosmetics and creams, and to candles and polishes for furniture, both of which were made from beeswax. All her recipes would be carefully recorded in the stillroom receipt book for the benefit of future generations.

Seemingly charming practices often concealed more mundane purposes: 'burning perfumes' and herbal vinegars were used to disinfect rooms; rue was strewn to ward off lice, while rosemary was used to keep moths away from linen. Soap had to be made from a coagulation of wood ash and mutton fat, so the addition of a strong fragrance would have been essential. (A batch of soap would have taken almost a day to make, so it is hardly surprising that washing was not considered a priority.)

7

Contents

Interest in the arts flourished during Elizabeth's reign. Singing, dancing, playing musical instruments, drama and poetry were all favourite pastimes of the Elizabethan gentleman and his family. Outdoors on the estate, his pursuits would have been hunting and falconry, while archery and bowls were garden activities.

Embroidery would be the chief pastime of the lady of the house, assisted by her servants. Between them they would undertake such daunting tasks as the embroidery of wall-hangings and heraldic panels, or the curtains, bedcovers and valances for the massive four-poster beds.

Subjects for embroidery ranged from interlacing patterns (which served for both needlework and knot-garden) through stylized stems and foliage, to figurative compositions incorporating flowers, fruits, insects and animals. Episodes from the Bible or classical mythology were often illustrated in a contemporary garden setting.

Gardening would undoubtedly have a place among the country gentleman's interests. Horticulture was still in its infancy, and many avenues were still to be explored. Science and myth were so hopelessly confused that the imagined possibilities of grafting and crossing plants made gardening a fascinating pastime.

For Chris

To plant strange country fruits, to sow such seeds likewise,
To dig and delve for new found roots, where old might well
suffice,
To prune the water boughs, to pick the mossy trees,
Oh how it pleased my fancy once to kneel upon my knees,
To griff a pippin stock, when sap begins to swell;
But since the gains scarce quit the cost, 'Fancy (quoth he)
farewell'.

FROM '*The Green Knight's Farewell to Fancy*' (1575),
By GEORGE GASCOIGNE

The Vertues

Flax 'The seeds stamped with the roots of wilde Cucumbers, draweth forth splinters, thornes, broken bones, or any other thing fixed in any part of the body.'

Mint 'It is poured into the eares with honie water. It is taken inwardly against Scolopenders, Beare-wormes, Sea-scorpions and serpents.'

Tobacco 'The drie leaves are used to be taken in a pipe set on fire and suckt into the stomacke, and thrust forth againe at the nosthrils against the pains of the head, rheumes (and) aches in any part of the body.'

Borage 'Syrrup made of the juice of Borage with sugar, adding thereto powder of the bone of a Stags heart, it is good against swouning, the cardiacke passion of the heart, against melancholy and the falling sicknesse.'

Stock Gillyflowers ' . . . are not used in Physicke, except amongst certaine Empericks and Quacksalvers, about love and lust matters which for modestie I omit.'

FROM GERARD'S *Herbal*, 1597.

The orchard was not maintained simply to supply fruit for the household, it was also a pleasure-garden, laid out ornamentally with the thoughtful provision of seats and arbours. For while the flower-garden was at its best for only a few weeks of the year, the fruit-trees blossomed in spring, were green and shady through the summer, and in autumn were more colourful than ever.

The Elizabethans were cautious of raw fruit which was suspected of causing almost any mysterious illness. However, cooked fruit was a different matter altogether, and was an ingredient in all kinds of pies, tarts and creamy puddings. Candied and preserved fruits were also considered harmless, as were marmalades and other sweet confections, served as part of the 'banquet'.

In gentlemen's orchards, newly-introduced fruits such as apricots, figs and peaches were grown alongside medlars, services, wardens and other medieval favourites which are no longer cultivated. It was an Irishman, Richard Harris, 'fruiterer to King Henry eight' who was largely responsible for the transformation of England's orchards when he introduced superior grafts from France and the Low Countries to his orchard in Kent, which in turn supplied others throughout the county. Kent has been known as 'the garden of England' ever since the reign of Elizabeth.

The Physick Herbs

'O, mickle is the powerful grace that lies
In plants, herbs, stones, and their true qualities;
For nought so vile that on the earth doth live
But to the earth some special good doth give.'

Romeo and Juliet.

The physick herbs were the most important plants in the garden; their cultivation, distillation and the preparation of medicines were among the housewife's many duties. No alternative to herbal medicine was known, so every ailment from warts to the bubonic plague had to be treated with a combination of plants and prayer. The names of many wild flowers betray their former place among the physick herbs, such as lungwort, liverwort, toothwort, throatwort and birthwort.

During Elizabeth's reign two outstanding herbals (books devoted to the study of plants) appeared. William Turner's *Herbal* of 1568 was followed less than thirty years later by an immense volume by John Gerard, in which every plant then grown or known in England was recorded. Among its entries were the many new plants introduced since Turner's work was published. It was widely held that all plants were of some benefit to man, and the 'temperature' and 'vertues' of every one were listed in early gardening books and herbals.

The Elizabethans spent many of their leisure hours in the garden, and their appreciation of its pleasures is evident from the poetry and literature of the day. Gardens were laid out like a series of outdoor rooms, each decorated and furnished with living plants and trees. Clipped knots and mazes, curious topiary figures, evenly-spaced fruit-trees and the orderly beds of the kitchen garden were all expressions of the Elizabethan love of pattern and symmetry.

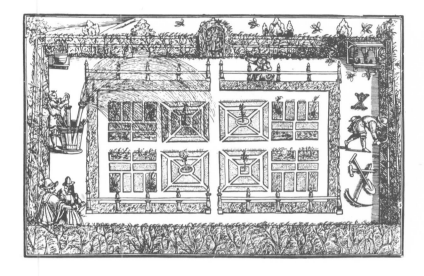

The Elizabethan Manor House

 BETWEEN 1570 and the Civil War in 1641, a great rebuilding took place all over England. New cottages, manors and mansions dotted the countryside, and many towns increased in size. The type of house illustrated by the model would probably be the home of a wealthy wool-merchant and his family. At that time it was possible for a prosperous yeoman, merchant or lawyer to join the ranks of the landed gentry simply by acquiring an estate and building an impressive house.

The house would be planned by the owner in consultation with his appointed master-craftsman, who would in turn commission others with specialist skills to work on details of woodwork, plasterwork and masonry. Houses were built with local materials, so the traditional half-timbered style continued to flourish in areas where wood was still plentiful.

The outward appearance of a house was of the utmost importance, as it displayed its owner's position and wealth to all who passed by. Whereas houses had formerly looked inward onto a courtyard, they now gazed out over surrounding gardens, which were designed as an integral part of the whole scheme.

'The life of man in this world is but a thraldom, when the sences are not pleased; and what rarer object can there bee on earth (the motions of the celestial bodies excepted) than a beautiful and odiferous Garden-plat Artificially composed, where he may read and contemplate on the wonderful works of the great Creator of plants and flowers; for if he observeth with a judicial eie, and a serious judgement their variety of Colours, Sents, Beautie, Shapes, Interlacing, Enamilling, Mixture, Turnings, Windings, Embossments, Operations and Virtues it is most admirable to behold and meditate upon the same.'

FROM *The Gardener's Labyrinth* By THOMAS HILL, 1571.

'It is a world also to see how many strange herbs, plants and annual fruits are daily brought into us from the Indies, Americas, Taprobane, Canary Isles and all parts of the world. . . . There is not almost one noble gentleman or merchant that hath not great store of these flowers, which now also begin to wax so well acquainted with our soils that we may almost account of them as parcel of our own commodities.'

FROM HARRISON'S *Description of England*, 1586-7.

10

The strict symmetry which is a feature of many Elizabethan houses marked a new approach to domestic building. Medieval manor houses had been fortified and functional, with little attention to style, although there were regional building traditions. With the 'great rebuilding' of the late sixteenth century, the style recognised today as Elizabethan gradually emerged. This combined various architectural features with a distinctive style of ornament inspired by classical Italian detail. In the hands of English rural craftsmen, it took on a character peculiar to England. Formerly essential features such as castellated parapets were also retained as decoration.

The model house is not based on a particular building (with the exception of the porch) but brings together some of the most typical features of the period, notably the mullion and transom windows, the bay windows, the gabled roof, the balustraded terraces and the central porch. Many ornate porches dating from Elizabeth's reign survive today; the one in the model is based on a particularly fine example found at Waterston Manor in Dorset. In the garden, the terraces and gazebos are symmetrically placed in relation to the house, and follow the same style.

'Make gum-water as strong as for Inke, but make it with Rose-water; then wet any growing flower therewith, about ten of the clock in a hot summers day, and when the Sun shineth bright, bending the flower so as you may dip it all over therein, and then shake the flower well; or else you may wet the flower with a soft callaver pencil, then strew the fine searced powder of double refined sugar upon it: do this with a little box or searce, whose bottom consisteth of an open lawn, and having also a cover on the top, holding a paper under each flower, to receive the sugar that falleth by: and in three houres it will candy or harden upon it; and so you may bid your friends after dinner to a growing banquet: or else you may cut off these flowers so prepared and dry them after in dishes two or three dayes in the sun, or by a fire, or in a stove; and so they will last six or eight weeks, happily longer, if they be kept in a place where the gum may not relent. You may do this also in Balme, Sage or Borrage, as they grow.'

FROM *Floraes Paradise*, By SIR HUGH PLAT, 1608.

15

Elizabethan 'sallets' were often served as a first course, and were eaten either raw or boiled, with oil, vinegar and pepper. Flowers such as primroses, violets, cowslips, borage flowers and others chosen for their scent or colour were sometimes strewn over the green 'sallet-herbs'. These might include lamb's lettuce, sorrel, succory, salad burnet, and many more we now regard as weeds.

Ingredients had to be carefully balanced, as an extreme in 'temperature' was believed to cause indigestion and various other complaints. A 'fiery' herb such as rocket or tarragon was tempered with lettuce, purslane or other 'cooling' herbs. Their effect could be modified by boiling, but raw sallets were not considered as harmful as uncooked fruit, since many of the herbs were also used for 'physick'. Caution was nevertheless advisable:

'And the often eating of Lettuce. is both dangerous to such women as be apt to conceive with childe, and such as be with child, for that . . . they do not onely cause barrennes, but those which then be with childe, shall after be delivered of children farre unlike their fathers, in that they shal be both raging of minde and foolishe in witte.'

FROM HILL'S *The Gardener's Labyrinth*, 1571.

The model illustrates some of the different types of knots: simplest of all were the 'open' knots, in which the area was filled with a pattern of raised flowerbeds, each edged with a low-growing shrub or herb and planted with flowers. More intricate 'closed' knots were formed by two or more interlacing threads, picked out in different evergreens. Often the spaces between them were coloured with a layer of 'dead' materials, such as coal-dust, brick-dust, sand or chalk. Alternatively, the threads might be edged with a double row of tiles and filled with flowers as directed in a book called *The English Husbandman*, published in 1613:

'Plant in every severall thread flowers of one kinde and colour, as thus for example: in one thread plant your carnation Gilly-flower, in another your great white Geli-flower, in another your mingle-coloured Gilly-flower, and in another your blood-red Gilly-flower . . . it shall appear like a knot made of divers coloured ribbons, most pleasing and most rare.'

Mazes were visual rather than three-dimensional puzzles, and sometimes appeared among the clipped evergreen designs of the knot-garden. One sixteenth-century gardening manual instructs the reader to grow one bed 'of cammomill, for to make seats and a labyrinth'. Bowling alleys were also sown with camomile, an aromatic herb which releases its scent when trodden upon.

'And because the Breath of Flowers is farre Sweeter in the Aire (where it comes and Goes, like the Warbling of Musick) then in the hand, therefore nothing is more fit for that delight, then to know, what be the Flowers, and Plants, that doe best perfume the Aire. Roses Damask and Red, are fast Flowers of their Smels; So that; you may walke by a whole Row of them, and finde Nothing of their Sweetnesse; Yea though it be, in a Mornings Dew. Bayes likewise yeeld no Smell, as they grow. Rosemary little; nor Sweet-Marioram. That, which above all Others, yeelds the Sweetest Smell in the Aire, is the Violet; Specially the White-double-Violet, which comes twice a Yeare; About the middle of Aprill, and about Bartholomew-tide. Next to that is, the Muske-Rose. Then the Strawberry-leaves dying, which (yeeld) a most Excellent Cordiall Smell . . . Then Wall-Flowers, which are very Delightfull, to be set under a Parler, or Lower Chamber Window. Then Pinks, (and Gilly-Flowers,) specially the Matted Pinck, and Clove Gilly-flower . . . But those which Perfume the Aire most delightfully, not passed by as the rest, but being Troden upon and Crushed, are Three: That is Burnet, Wilde-Time, and Water-Mints. Therefore, you are to set whole Allies of them, to have the Pleasure, when you walke or tread.'

FROM *'Of Gardens', The Essayes* By FRANCIS BACON, 1625.

'If many seedes of the Leekes be tyed up togither, and soone after watered, then will all the seedes in an heape togither, grow up into one marvellous bigge Leeke right wonderous to beholde.

'And if you will have the leaves of the Parcely grow crisped, then before the sowing of them, stuffe a tenis ball with the seedes, and beat the same wel against the ground, Whereby the seedes may so be a little brused, and then sowe them in the ground. . . .

'And to make divers formes like to birdes or beasts, and sundry perfit letters (of ye Romain fashion) on your Gourdes, or Cucumbers, then take the yong fruite of either, as the same groweth on the braunches, inclosing it into a molde of the like bignesse to the fruite, in the which, let be imprinted deep or holowe, in the forme that you desire to have after on your Gourde or Cucumber, and the like shall then appeare when as the fruite is come to his full growth and bignesse.

FROM *The Gardener's Labyrinth* By THOMAS HILL, 1571.

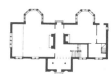

Although the outward appearance of the Elizabethan house was noticeably different, the interior still followed the medieval plan. The main entrance would open into a dividing passage known as the 'screens'. On one side would be the Hall, a vast room in which the whole household dined together. The Squire and his family occupied an elevated dais at the far end, beyond which lay the parlour and main staircase.

Above the parlour would be the principal room of the house, known as the Great Chamber, where the Squire would receive his guests. Also on this floor would be the bedchambers, and (in the larger houses) the Long Gallery, so called because it ran the whole length of the building.

Downstairs, on the other side of the screens passage, would be doors leading to the kitchen, pantry, buttery and other household offices. As the external symmetry of the house was not yet echoed within, a feature such as a bay window planned for the dais or parlour would have to be repeated in one of these lesser rooms.

Almost every Elizabethan garden would have had an arbour, framed with wooden poles and overgrown with climbing plants such as honeysuckle and eglantine. Sometimes, continuous arbours called galleries were constructed, and these formed shady tunnels opening out onto the garden.

During summer it was customary for the country gentleman and his guests to adjourn to the garden after dinner for the 'banquet', which was the final course of the meal. This was usually served in an arbour, although some larger houses boasted a purpose-built banqueting house. As Justice Shallow says in Henry IV, Part 2:

'Nay, you shall see mine orchard where in an arbour, we will eat a last year's pippin of mine own grafting with a dish of carraways and so forth.'

12

Elizabethan gardeners were skilled in the art of topiary. Their creations usually took shape in rosemary: box and yew were more popular in the seventeenth century when clipping became a mania and topiary reached heights of invention. The following excerpt is taken from Thomas Platter's description of the gardens at Hampton Court in 1599:

'They were all manner of shapes, men and women, half men and half horse, sirens, serving-maids with baskets, French lilies and delicate crenellations all round made from dry twigs bound together and the aforesaid evergreen quickset shrubs, or entirely of rosemary, all true to the life, and so cleverly and amusingly interwoven, mingled and grown together, trimmed and arranged picture-wise, that their equal would be difficult to find.'

Mounts were originally constructed within castle walls, giving a view over the surrounding countryside, and thus warning of an enemy approach. William Lawson suggests a more tranquil way of life in his book, *A New Orchard and Garden*, published in 1618:

'In my opinion, I could highly recommend your orchard, if either through it or hard by it there should run a pleasant river with silver streams. You might sit in your Mount and angle a peckled Trout, sleighty Eele, or some other dainty Fish.'

13

Furnishings

Although Elizabethan interiors were very basic, every available surface was decorated; ceilings were patterned with intricate plasterwork, while walls were lined with carved oak panelling, tapestries and embroidered hangings. Carpets were draped over tables rather than spread on floors, which were paved or tiled downstairs and wooden on the upper storeys. Aromatic herbs were strewn on the floors to counteract the damp and musty smell of the rooms, and little bags of pot-pourri hung about the house for the same purpose. Dr Lemnus, a Dutch visitor to England in 1560, was impressed:

' . . . their chambers and parlours strawed over with sweete herbs refreshed me; their nosegayes finely intermingled with sundry sorte of fragraunte floures in their bedchambers and privy rooms with comfortable smell cheered me up and entirely delighted all my senses.'

Even the chief rooms were very sparsely furnished. The few pieces in each were of solid oak and elaborately carved. There would have been chests, tables, stools, benches and of course the enormous four-poster beds, which, with the curtains drawn, became rooms in themselves. Chairs were a symbol of status, and there would have been at the most only two in the entire house – one for the owner, the other for his wife.

4

Secrets of Sowing and Planting

'A marvellous matter of the Basill, that if the seedes be sowen with cursed wordes, lyke as men commonly doe in the sowing of Hemp-seede, that then they will come up the better, and the sooner.

'And the Artichokes will growe without prickles if that the sharpe endes be pressed downe, or made blunt by rubbing them on a stone, before the setting in the earth. . . .

'And that many savours and tastes may be felt in one herbe; take first of the lettuce two or three seedes, of the Endive so many, of the Smallache the like, of the Basill, of the Leeke, and of the Percely, . . . then put all the seedes into a hole togither, and in such sort that the seedes may touch one another; but this before remembred, that you put them togither in the dung of a horse or oxe, without any earth mingled with them. And thus sowne, there will after spring up a plant, having so manie savours or tastes, as there were seedes sowne togither.'

FROM *The Gardener's Labyrinth* By THOMAS HILL, 1571.

21